CW00505603

APOLOGY
for
ABSENCE

Apology
for
Absence

JULIA DARLING

PUBLICATIONS
2004

Published by Arc Publications
Nanholme Mill, Shaw Wood Road
Todmorden, Lancs OL14 6DA

Design by Tony Ward
Printed by Antony Rowe Ltd.,
Eastbourne, E. Sussex

ISBN 1 904614 12 4

Acknowledgments:
The author's love and special thanks go to
Jackie Kay, Linda France, Cynthia Fuller,
Linda Anderson and Ann Spencer and
Emma Holliday for her paintings
that inspired 'Two Lighthouses',
'Rendez Vous Café' and 'The Hollow'.

The publishers acknowlege
financial assistance from the
Arts Council of England, Yorkshire.

Editor, UK & Ireland: Jo Shapcott

Dedicated to
Bev, Scarlet and Florrie,
and to the memory of my friend
Andrea Badenoch

CONTENTS

VISUALISATION

You are on a path, leading to the blue wood,
you are floating. Everything you touch shivers
then blossoms. You have perfect knees, glossy hair.
You are sure of your destination (breathe deeply).
You pass a waterfall spilling from a cave
and an elegant fish leaps from the water.
See its rainbow scales. A kingfisher hovers.
Go to the bank, put your hand in the water.
Pure, ice cold water. Wipe it on your lips.
It tastes of honey and elderflower. Drink deeply.
This water will cure you, feel its cool fire
soaking into your bones. You are strong.
Stay there, with the birdsong, don't open your eyes,
for a wrathful cat sits on your chest.
and your sheets need washing.
Stay with the path. Keep the nettles trimmed.
Don't think of liver fluke. Try to be American.

WAYS OF DISCUSSING MY BODY

I am a cow, when her calves are taken,
mooing by the gate, with muddy knees.
I'm a woodshed before the explosion,
a swollen kite, pulling at a string.

A giraffe with a narrow and fragile neck,
a still life that's shabbily arranged,
a badly made stool that won't stand up.
I'm that pair of uncomfortable shoes.

I'm a soldier, a veil. I'm a wardrobe.
Do you understand me? I am not what you see.
I am buried at the bottom of a lake.
My parts are many and they don't match.

LIVING IN THE MOMENT

Each moment has edges,
ultimatums, rules.
You can live
in its temporary rooms.

Some moments glitter,
they land in my arms,
red dawns, wild epiphanies.
I have gathered them all,

and stored the best ones
in the safest places
for I may need these moments,
when the present tumbles.

THIS IS A DAY OF SOUP

Luckily, this is a day of soup,
of still surfaces, of back burners,
a day of turning to the small print
and running my finger down a list.
Not a day of suitcases, like yesterday,
of testing handles, the smoothness of wheels,
or a day of corners, steps and slopes.
Last week was all dark tunnels
and lost appointments, fluttering like birds.
Some days are too hot to touch.
I have to wear armour, goggles, gloves.
Tomorrow could be a blind summit.
But today is thick with pearl barley,
lentil and tinned tomato. Today is deliberate,
nutritious. It will take hours,
require a deep bowl, a balanced spoon.

INJECTION

Brown walls. The clip and gleam of hospitals.
Here I am again, having scans, being told
to roll up my sleeve, be still.

And here he is, a freckled man, jabbing at my
hardened arteries, not listening when I say
not that one, that one's dead.

He fails to draw blood, disappears.

In walks a woman with headmistress eyes.
'This one's a squealer,' says the nurse,
 so she sighs, rears up with a needle.

I just want to howl for mercy,
to gulp and scream, tell my story,
again and again. Make them sit still, listen.

THE WATER EXTRACTOR

I can't stop thinking about
the water extractor Ann mentioned
as she was going out of the door,
that sucked the moisture out of rooms.

I have tried to imagine
its shape, its vast, thirsty tongue,
the sound of its vibrant recesses,
how it knows not to take everything.

Apparently many machines
are available for hire. Extraordinary.
What other machines are there?
Where is the catalogue?

I would like a spiritual cleanser,
an automatic comforter,
a sushi maker, a cat groomer,
a bath essence maker,

a polisher for my arterial corridors,
a machine for blasting rooms with mirth,
a portable bone strengthener,
and a fear shrinker, one for every room.

GETTING THERE

The yellow number one bus didn't stop
so I crossed the street, boarded a single decker
that lurched out of the ordinary timetable,
faced steep lanes, and terrible bends
that no regular bus could foresee.
I clung to my imagination, my buttons.
My companions had loud conversations
and frail bodies. They hung on, bravely,
as the bus swerved and screamed,
keeled like a boat, shuddered, growled.
We went backwards, we stopped, started.
The bus was filled with leftover people
from other bus routes, other destinations.
We shared toffees. One woman sang.
It was an exuberant, unlikely bus.
The journey to the city took so long,
as we made a thousand detours.
I felt that I had seen the universe,
its heights and depressions. I was bruised,
dented with corners, but when I stepped down
the earth beneath my feet felt older, stronger.

EMAIL

How are you? I had a test, but they couldn't find
    the vein.
How's your pain? Mine's not bad. At night I sweat.
Have you tried those apricot kernels yet?
Mine's round my rib. It hasn't reached the lungs.
Soft is bad. That's what he implied. I'm thinking
if I ignore it , I won't die.

My acupuncturist says I'm doing well.

Afterwards I ate four kiwi, rode my bike.
We always left parties early didn't we? I don't like
hanging round too long. I'm really glad we won't
    be old
and dribbling in a stair lift, wearing pads.
Have you tried prayer? I never thought I would,
but lately I've forgiven everyone. It's good.

PROBABLY SUNDAY

One daughter is sleeping, her face unbuttoned.
She's dreaming of wardrobes, of sharp gold shoes.

Downstairs her mother writes her will
and studies investments, orders the past.

And the mother's lover is at the computer
shooting dragons and snakes in a watery cave.

Another daughter runs a manicured finger
down a list of queens, memorising their deaths.

The dog barks in the hallway and the cat
examines a spider, then kills it.

We are baking potatoes, it's probably Sunday.
We are an English family in an endless terrace.

SALSA DANCING CLASS. HEATON.

These men that try to dance, whose necks
are wiry red, for whom the steps are
clear as mud. They have a dream

to take off pullovers and swirl, to get
a girl with silver shoes, a jingly belt
which shimmies when she spins. Ah men.

I'm just as bad. I'm stiff meat. But, Mambo beat
I will tame you, flex myself into your Latin
scrum. I've been sofa bound too long,

too fond of being weakly, English pale.
Is it impossible to glow, to wriggle
my backside, click my tongue?

And is it sad, post menopause, to have a whim
to stop doing the aimless Sapphic stomp?
I'll practise, get videos, do anything

to feel a surge, pull out a miracle,
find my Brazil, wake up in Cuba,
plug myself in. Stop counting.

LARGE OLD MEN

The large old men are dancing at a disco
with their wild hands and bowl stomachs.

They stagger amongst the giggly girls
boulders in a river, fallen walls.

They have memories as long as fishing lines
and salt marks on their drooping cheeks.

They are still alive and floating,
bobbing, trying to catch the moths

above their heads, or waving at the lost
children at the end of the path.

Stamping on the envelopes that came
without warning, those bad letters.

The large old men are dancing at a disco
with their bare faces turned inside out.

PHONE CALL FROM THE HOSPICE

You know when it's Sunday
because the chef isn't here.

Other days are the same,
Pop Idol, magazines.

They fiddle with drugs,
then the visitors come.

Don't worry. I'll get out.
We'll go to Dumfries,

walk down that bright path
to Saint Ninian's Cave,

scratch our names on stones
and place them there.

WHEN I WAS HEALTHY THINGS WERE OFTEN YELLOW

I walked into a town filled with bananas.
The main street was one long banana stall.
It was sweet, rotting, like being
in a milkshake, or being mashed
with a fork, turning brown, ripening.

And I lay on a rug, on pale yellow sand;
dune grass whipped my shins,
the sea was a long devouring wave,
I threw a piece of driftwood shaped
like a sleeping yellow snake.

I was holding a wounded dandelion,
dripping dandelion milk. Its silky head
trembled with a hazy halo of prongs.
It was telling me the time. Buttercups
were knee deep then. Cows were vocal.

I dream of straw, of horse milk,
of the primrose path to the wood,
the vanilla wafer that slipped away.
And fear, a heavy bee against the window,
the tyranny of that ridiculously cheerful sun.

TURN OFF THE LIGHTS WHEN YOU GO TO BED

I am the woman who wears reading glasses
listening at the top of the stairs.

I am keeping an eye on your movements,
I know what you eat. I note

the number of hours you sleep, how much
television you watch. I am the night matron

and the day nurse. I hold the keys to your childhood.
I am your worrier. How I worry about your future.

I mould it like clay, but it falls
into pieces in my hands. I tell you be careful,

again and again I say it. Be careful.
Turn off the lights when you go to bed.

Then I monitor your dreams. Madness.
How I wish I would leave you alone.

PARENTING

First you were born then
mashed banana turning brown
Barbi's decapitated head
Ken's torso tangled Lego
journeys South a promised sea
adjusting the mirror
share your sweets, sing, sing
wading down copper rivers
wet socks a snow scape out of salt
a door wide open calling down the street
are you coming in, are you, are you?
a gaggle of girls at a bus stop
a bleeding knee wet cotton wool
where's it gone? I want, I want
wrinkled balloons bumping over the grass
at the school fair, primary pastry
clean the paint brushes or they go stiff
a pancake flies into the air
the other mothers in their coats
are you picking up? Or is it me?
sugar oats ribbon rolling eggs
in bed watching Oliver
be quiet go to sleep wake up
a clarinet solo in a school play
that's her, she's mine
crabs in a bucket the boat in the harbour
wiping the kitchen table again and again
fasten your seat belt

passing my credit card across
the supermarket check out
signing my name
is that ms or mrs?
many pets all dead
did I tell you I love you?
come back here now!
Then you left.

IMPOSSIBLE

to understand the way a teenager hears questions,
like a whine, disturbing their inner hum.
You have forgotten it, that itching ache.
And the teenager thinks everyone is looking.
It makes them feel as if their limbs are swaddled
and so they hunch their shoulders, lower eyes,
leave the tap running, the top off, slam the door.
They cry, then laugh. They eat without looking
and don't notice the washing in the rain.
You point out that the sink is blocked,
dislike the way they won't keep still.
You want them to be sorry, feel remorse.
But that's impossible, don't you understand?
Because nothing fits, because life is electric,
tomorrow tastes of sherbet, and the night
whirs round them like a moth, and you
just stand there with your rolled up paper
trying to stop the fluttering, the buzz.

APOLOGY FOR ABSENCE

Look, it's as if my heart is a damp cupboard
filled with old brass that needs polishing.

Or I must cover myself with moss, damp down,
try to establish new growth in the rotting.

Sometimes I am whipped to shreds by the North wind
and must curl up beneath a counterpane.

I need to practise dying, to imagine health,
to eat tinned pears, light unnecessary fires.

And love can be tyrannical, so sweet, yet edgy.
I am overpowered by its fragrant red roses.

Sitting rooms are too vivid. Things get torn.
I have to disappear, to darn each rip.

Forgive me, brave daughters, for the questions
that I have failed to answer. And my love,

please don't say I malingered, don't be
angry later, when you add up the ticks.

AFTER ALL THAT

And then the rooms are empty.
There's a sock on the floor,
a moon-shaped slither of soap,
used cotton wool buds by the bath.

And I have many things to do,
my wiping up, my polishing.
But then, it is also finished
and there is nothing to do.

Why would I want to plant nasturtiums?
For whom am I making a bright garden?
There is nothing I want in the shops.
What is the point of cake?

MY DAUGHTERS READING IN MAY

I love the smell of my daughters reading
as they turn the pages, pushing hair behind ears,
especially in this early Summer, with its fat leaves
new and surprised, the trees full of juice
and so many dandelions, so much yellow.
The downy light touches their heads,
their bodies untangle on the long red sofa;
they have forgotten mirrors, clothes, tomorrow.
I could touch their cheeks, as if they were babies,
for they hardly see me as I walk past them.
I can hang in the air, like a comma, breathing,
as their stories unravel, and the afternoon purrs.

SATISFACTORY

The hawthorn outside is shocked with blossom
as we eat a large breakfast. They've got off a ferry,
hair in thin plaits, bent double with rucksacks
as if they still carry the weight of childhood.

Who knows where they've been, with their heavy
tents, and whose mud is crusted on their shoes.
I might pass them in corridors, they wouldn't see me.
They speak a new language of pauses and barks.

I am learning the art of not enquiring,
What is that bruise upon your neck?
Have a tomato. Close the door when you go.
I am off to discover the meaning of ants.

DAYS OF TERRIBLE TIREDNESS

These short days, when I try too hard
to get there, to make myself,

to sit and push, to pull in words,
pull up weeds, take vitamin C,

to pedal, to arrive, think it through,
to write my lists, tie up ends;

I think sometimes it's finished now,
this endless drive, this pacing on.

I think sometimes I might just sleep
wrapped in fur, close my brown eyes,

be washed away, be satisfied
with this and what it always was.

SLEEPING IN MARCH

I slept through March; its needling winds
drove me to my bed where I lay with radio plays

and evaporated breath, buttoned in sleep's drowsy coat,
hands clasped on my chest, stone fingers.

I dreamt of missed appointments, failed exams,
while my body folded itself, darned the tears,

sides to middle. Whenever I opened my eyes
the light was fading, only clouds moved.

I felt guilty, as if I was floating out to sea
on a stolen raft, as if my old headmistress

was calling *you lazy girl, you're drifting again,
you're not even wearing a beret!* I ignored it all.

I slept through March, and rose in April.
My skin had lost its creases. I had new eyes.

SEPTEMBER POEM

On my new bike I will swerve round your corners
dodge your lights, make one way my way.

I'll be a leaf, a glossy conker on a string,
a bright red berry that looks surprised.

Think I'll start a bonfire, smoke all day
eat blackberry pie, pickle those onions,

hold my trousers up with string, pull
the frayed cuffs of my pullover. Suck wool.

This September joy, an alarming hope,
strong as cider, even though I'm shivering,

smelling the chill, so I keep wheeling
warding it off, whistling, pretending

I have never been cold. Never afraid,
never had to cross the ice.

NIGHT SWEAT

You wake up with your face melting,
an evangelical bird calling you,
the sky dripping with loss.

You claim to be asleep.
Your eyes are closed. Your breath
plods round your chest.

You attempt to plead
with night. You make a promise.
You say that if he lets you go

you'll give him all your furniture,
sew up the arm holes in your clothes,
donate your family to science.

Night covers up your mouth
and nestles in your hair.
He says you have till dawn,

after which he expects results.
The straw must be spun into gold
and you must be able to answer.

MY COMPLICATED DAUGHTER

What can I do for my complicated daughter,
my terror, my dark heart, so lost in this house?
Where can we meet? On the stairs, on the landing?
At night as we dream? In the bold brass of day?
If only I could make her a cagoule of rescue,
heal all her scars, wrap her sore life in silk,
or bury her pain at the end of the garden
with my bare hands. I'd give her a sack full of wishes.
But she will not hear me, and I cannot see her.
We collide in the bathroom, by the terrible mirror,
so apart, so unable to give or receive.

LISTENING TO JACK LISTENING TO MUSIC

After bedtime she closes the door and turns up Joni,
or Kathleen, or Ella. She communes with Nina.

I can hear her chinking, looking into the glass,
searching between notes for a path into night.

She's a party, an orchestra, a clamour and hush,
sweet, jazz thoughts rise and fall. It's their hour,

she's conducting, shushing them, putting them straight.
She won't take them to bed. They might never untangle.

I hear her minors, her majors, her magnificent solos.
Inside the fridge champagne pops by itself.

I am upstairs, dreaming, hearing that magic,
those embers, those divas, singing her home.

NURSES

Slope shouldered, bellies before them,
the nurses are coming, garrulously,
they are bossing me in and out of clothes
into windowless rooms, tucking me in.
Nurses are patting me, frowning,
then they guffaw in another room.
They have flat footed footsteps
and very short memories.

But I am the woman who won't take off her bra,
the one who demands that you look in her eyes.
Miss Shirty, they call me, I know my own veins;
when they come back for me, I'll be gone.

WEIGHT

I am weighed down by carrier bags
of duty, cans of obligation.

A bowl sky sags above my head.
It's like sitting in a tent in the rain.

These blankets are as heavy as cows.
My bones are fossilised trees.

I am clogged up with sympathy,
so that nothing turns or whirrs,

but some things are never onerous
like you in your white ironed shirt

bringing the tea in the morning, quietly
whispering, *sleep, if you want to, sleep.*

TWO LIGHTHOUSES

I would like us to live like two lighthouses
at the mouth of a river, each with her own lamp.

We could see each other across the water,
which would be dangerous, and uncrossable.

I could watch your shape, your warm shadow,
moving in the upper rooms. We would have jokes.

Jokes that were only ours, signs and secrets,
flares on birthdays, a rocket at Christmas.

Clouds would be cities, we would look for omens,
and learn the impossible language of birds.

We would meet, of course, in cinemas, cafes,
but then, we would return to our towers,

knowing the other was the light on the water,
a beam of alignment. It would never be broken.

RENDEZ-VOUS CAFÉ: WHITLEY BAY

I would like us to meet
where the Horlicks is sweet.

I could tell you my story
with a knickerbocker glory.

Talk of mermaids all day
spooning pear parfait.

Licking ninety-nine cones
we could turn off our phones.

Smile, perhaps disappear,
with a chocolate éclair.

Rendez -vous with the sea
and the sugary breeze.

Come eat strawberry flan
while we can, while we can.

OLD JEZZY

I went to old Jesmond Graveyard
to find my plot, to mark a place.
Doug from Bereavement showed me a spot
green and reflective, under a willow.
He apologised for the trimming of weeds,
he liked it messy, overgrown,
but the government had made stipulations
for health and safety, things must be neat,
in case of gravestones squashing children,
so raggy old Jezzy was having a clean up.
But you know, said Doug, death isn't tidy.
It's a plague of knotweed, a bed of nettles,
a path through thistles, that's how it should be.

A SHORT MANIFESTO FOR MY CITY

This city shall treasure its pedestrians
and its small places, its irregular shops.

It shall hang onto its pink lanes, its towers,
Dog Leap stairs and Pudding Chares.

And the city shall never try to be Barcelona,
or dress itself in luxury underwear.

Let it be salty, and rusty with iron,
keep secrets beneath its potent river

and be proud to be radical, afraid
of refurbishment. It doesn't need fireworks,

or Starbucks; for it knows its interior.
Let it always be ready to take off its hat.

My city is hard stone, canny and clever.
Don't give it a mirror. Let it be itself.

MY THUMB IN LEEDS

My thumb is on holiday. It hooks itself
around a key, unlocks a hotel bedroom door.

It lies in green water and softens.
It flicks the remote, orders room service,

says thank you, enjoys being licked.
My thumb puts on its best gloves.

It rides in my pocket. It's pink,
enthusiastic. My thumb takes photographs.

At the art gallery it touches sculptures,
resolves to take up painting, feels my fingers.

Holds a cup of cappuccino, touches clothes
on rails in Harvey Nichols. My thumb sighs.

It carries the cases home, grips on tight.
That's all a thumb can do. Hold on.

MOVING TO THE COUNTRY

We are always looking at for sale signs
down leafy lanes, imagining ourselves
freed from sirens, the clank of the city.
We try to see ourselves in fields
with large deep freezes, happily
wearing floppy hats, with secateurs.
We hope that we would fit in,
with our urban graces, our town shoes,
though the village people scowl
and have thick fingers, hang dead birds
from barbed wire fences.
We would try to trust the animals,
who seem so furious and dim.
We would ignore the crows,
that arrange themselves like omens.
We always end up driving home, relieved
full of scone, saying we would miss the cinema.

COAT

so I open the door and the air smells
of snails and unwashed flannels and I am
unsure what coat to wear for I might
be too hot in my Macintosh or perhaps
rain will slither down my neck in a jacket
so I turn back and go to my wardrobe
and contemplate the rows of coats I keep
huddled like old women waiting for an outing
for I have so many unworn coats

HOLLOW

From the high bed I can see nothing but blossom,
Good Friday light, with a pale egg sky.

It's a simple day, like that flower in a blue vase.
I am a long way from a supermarket car park.

Here in the hollow, with the lull of wood pigeons,
in the open palm of another woman's history.

THE RECOVERY BED

I am lying on a bed in the debatable lands,
considering matters of queenly importance.

The room has two windows, and from each I see
the far far horizon, the reclining hills.

And the bed is decisive, with fine brass bed knobs
and a heavy quilt. It's a bed of grace.

There's no one here. I am able to lie
all day, if necessary, letting my life

fly past like the birds, rise and fall as the clouds;
I am riding a raft that was made by kind women

who have left me here, who gave me a key,
for I was forgetting to look out of the window, but now,

I shall float home, firm as this mattress.
You will find me quite sure, convalesced.

MY OLD FRIEND HOSPITAL

You know the cadence of my footsteps now,
and I am intimate with your sighs,
those humming lifts, your fluttering blinds,
your Fionas, Paulines, Marilyns and Dots,
your, *this might hurt, there, all done,*
the swish of your trolleys, your cotton arms,
strolling doctors, the fridge that's full of juice,
the purr of the green curtains pulled
round the bed, the sauntering ward clerks
carrying my thick, buff coloured files,
while my temperature rises and then falls.
Whoever would have thought
I might love a hospital, but I do:
you know me now, and I know you.

IT'S NEARLY TIME

to pull on socks again. A wind
blows exhausted teacloths on the line.
They flap and flap,

and all the fields and trees
are wrung out. Their colour has
drained into the earth.

The sky's a sheet in an Oxfam shop
with grim stains shaped
like warring countries.

We must cover up red varnished toes
and hammer down the days
cut things back to stubs,

examine bolts and catches,
stock up on anti ageing cream,
Solpadine, and learn some jokes.

HEARING THINGS

I heard my insides first, an alarming hum
of swelling pipes, the glug of blood
around my heart, the gestetner of my brain,
wrench of intestine, whine of bones.

I listened further, to the silence
at the heart of everyone, that wide lake
with guarded fences. I tried to catch
the fishes breathing, bubbles from the deep.

Then, yesterday, in my front room, I heard
the tearing sound of children leaving home.
At the bus stop, there was music in the folds
of a pensioners skirt, and the high

pitched squeak of longing, a teenager
who held her silent mobile phone
and yearned for it to ring. I wish
that I could hear the future, but I can't.

IT'S NOT OVER

A walk you thought was over
opens into a miraculous valley.
You're in your stride.
You've thrown away
the map and you
could walk forever.

The bush that died
now leaps with blossom,
as if it's dressing for the Oscars.
It isn't cowed by Winter, or
newsmen who call through sand
The world is ending!

This is the epic last chapter
the firework that won't
go out, it just keeps spinning.
After the coffees, they bring out
a chocolate mermaid!
a pyramid of ice!

Glorious undead drunks
still flail and croon
down Northumberland Street.
They dance for England.
Oddly, it's not over yet.
This is the best bit.

INDELIBLE, MIRACULOUS

friend, think of your breath
on a cold pane of glass

you can write your name there
with an outstretched finger

or frosted, untouched grass
in the early morning, a place

where you can dance alone
leave your footprints there

a deep pool of silver water
waits for you to make waves

the beach is clean after the storm
the tide has washed away yesterday

we all matter, we are all
indelible, miraculous, here

ABOUT THE AUTHOR

Julia Darling has lived in Newcastle upon Tyne since 1980 and began her writing career as a poet, working with a performance group 'The Poetry Virgins' for many years, 'taking poetry to the places that least expected it'.

In 1988 her first novel *Crocodile Soup* was published by Anchor at Transworld. The novel went on to be published in Canada, Australia, Europe and the United States and was long-listed for the Orange Prize. Her most recent novel, *The Taxi Driver's Daughter*, was published by Penguin and long-listed for the Man Booker Prize and short-listed for the Encore Award. She has also written many plays for stage and radio, including *Posties* for Radio 4's 'Woman's Hour' and *Manifesto for the New City* for Northern Stage.

In 2003, Julia Darling's first full-length collection of poems, *Sudden Collapses in Public Places*, was published by Arc and was awarded a Poetry Book Society Recommendation.

She is currently Fellow of Literature and Health in the English School at Newcastle University and is a recipient of the acclaimed Northern Rock Foundation Writer's Award, the largest annual literary award in England. She is also working on a new novel for Penguin.

To find out more about her work, or to read her weblog, go to www.juliadarling.co.uk.

Recent publications in
Arc Publications' series
POETRY FROM THE UK / IRELAND
edited by Jo Shapcott
include:

LIZ ALMOND
The Shut Drawer

JONATHAN ASSER
Outside The All Stars

DONALD ATKINSON
In Waterlight:
Poems New, Selected & Revised

JULIA DARLING
Sudden Collapses in Public Places

CHRISSIE GITTINS
Armature

JOEL LANE
Trouble in the Heartland

HERBERT LOMAS
The Vale of Todmorden

IAN POPLE
An Occasional Lean-to

SUBHADASSI
peeled

JACKIE WILLS
Fever Tree